Work is a significant part of your life.
Why not make it better?

You can.

This book shows you how to get
more success and more meaning from
work. And it lays out a short, easy-to-follow
plan to make it happen.

Soon you can Make Work Better.

ISBN 978-1-484-98269-3

Published in the United States by CreateSpace.com

To order additional copies contact:
service@virtueswork.com

Make Work Better

Alexander Cummings

Make Work Better

I. Make your time at work better

Work is one of your life's great projects. And like all your other great projects, you have hopes and dreams about work—what you want to do, the path your career will take, etc. This book will show you how to make your time at work better, and, at the same time, help your dreams come true. As you will see, it's easy to do.

Making work better for most people means having more success and more fulfillment at work. Success means being rewarded for your effort. Maybe with money, but certainly with recognition and respect. And fulfillment means doing something important—something that matters, not just punching a clock.

The success that you want—the success that separates you from your peers—comes from having high-level skills, strategic skills and "soft" skills. Skills such as good judgment, keen analysis, effective leadership, etc. This book will show you a powerful tool that can give you these skills. But the tool does more than that. This tool can make every aspect of your work better. What is this tool? The virtues. And virtues make work better.

Management professors have recognized the benefits of using the virtues at work. Jim Collins, in his best-selling management book *Good to Great,* discusses the importance of virtues in helping companies outperform their competitors. And Professor Jeffery Sonnenfeld at Yale University, an expert on leadership, has identified five elements that make an effective leader and four of them are virtues.

It might come as a surprise, but opportunities to use the virtues come up frequently at work. For example, on September 11, 2001, Jimmy Dunne worked for a small investment bank. He was one of three executives on a committee that ran the firm. That day he was playing golf instead of working at the company's World Trade Center headquarters. Sixty-six of the firm's 83 World Trade Center employees died that day, including the two other executives that ran the company— more than one-third of the whole firm. After 9/11 Dunne struggled to keep the firm open. But he decided to keep paying the salaries of all those killed. He paid them until the end of the year, and then paid them all their bonuses, making sure that year's bonus equaled or exceeded the highest bonus ever received by that employee. And any new commissions on accounts opened before September 11th went to the victims' family until the end of the year, rather than the person who now managed the account. And the firm pledged to pay the health insurance for any victims' survivors for years. Dunne used the virtue of compassion at work.

Most opportunities to use the virtues at work aren't as dramatic as Jimmy Dunne's. Rather, most opportunities come up in your day-to-day interactions and decisions. They are treasure hidden in plain sight. And whether the opportunity is big or small, the virtues can have a significant impact on you and your time at work.

II. What are the virtues? What can they do for me?

A virtue is a habit that develops the good within you.

Plato and Aristotle wrote about the virtues. So did St. Thomas Aquinas, Adam Smith and Benjamin Franklin. These thinkers were concerned with man's goal in life and how to achieve it. They all focused on the virtues because the virtues are built on the truths about human nature and what makes us happy.

St. Thomas Aquinas developed an influential framework for understanding the virtues. He identified many habits that develop the good within you, but described seven principal virtues. Altered slightly for the workplace they are:

1. Compassion
2. Justice
3. Prudence
4. Courage
5. Self-control
6. Humility
7. Hope

These seven virtues affect all aspects of your life, including your work. Compassion and justice are focused outward; they determine how you treat others, which affects your relationships and reputation. The other virtues—of which prudence is the most important—do their work within you. They change what drives your actions. They replace whim or emotion with facts and reason. This leads to smarter decisions at work.

As you will see, success comes from skills that develop as you use the virtues. What kinds of skills? The virtues can help you make better decisions, take the initiative, inspire others, and master other high value-added skills necessary for success.

Besides helping you with skills, the virtues save you from serious problems. You will develop self-destructive habits if you don't use the virtues; destructive habits such as indecisiveness, cowardice, recklessness, etc. These sabotage your efforts at success and deprive your work of meaning. As you will see, every virtue prevents you from falling into specific self-destructive habits.

To use the virtues and get their rewards you need to do two things. One, use your reason and will. When you use your reason, you know what the best thing to do is, and your will gets you to do it. You become smart and disciplined, a powerful combination.

And second, to use the virtues fully, focus on something outside of yourself. This shift in focus away from yourself always gives your work more meaning. "Man finds happiness only in serving others," wrote Leo Tolstoy. When done for someone—or something—else your work becomes fulfilling, something you want to do.

As you see, the virtues are grounded in fundamental truths about human nature, they strengthen some of the powerful abilities that you have been given, and they focus on the root causes of your behavior. That is why they can make deep, lasting changes and have a greater impact on you and your time at work than the advice found in work-oriented self-help books.

Some virtues will come easily or naturally to you. But even with those, virtues only become habits when you repeat them, use them whenever the opportunity arises. According to Aristotle, all virtues and vices are voluntary. You choose to use a virtue. Once they are habits it may be an unconscious choice, but it is a choice. There is always a pull or temptation away from the virtues, but if you use your reason and will to choose to use the virtues, skills and success can follow. And you can make your time at work better.

III. That sounds good, but...

Some people think that the virtues aren't appropriate for their organization or industry. They are wrong. Research published in *The Wall Street Journal* reports that one person in a group who acts contrary to the virtues—"lazy," "obnoxious" or "excessively critical"—can cut the group's performance by 40%. Worse, this kind of negative behavior is highly "contagious." No organization is better off when its workers can't cooperate and shirk their duties.

And some shy away from the virtues because they think that they will be the only one using them. Not so. More and more organizations allow workers to develop their character or faith at work. *The New York Times, The Wall Street Journal, Fortune* and others have written about companies that have chaplains, set aside space for employee prayer, hold Bible study classes, etc. This is spreading because it is good for workers and, therefore, for the organization. When you use the virtues at work you are part of this progressive trend. And to make it easier to be part of this trend, remember that the virtues have concrete, tangible benefits for you and your organization.

Some people wonder if the virtues are necessary, citing the people at work who don't use the virtues but are successful. Their success comes from an ability or good habit that they have (hard work, for example). But if they don't use the virtues, they will develop self-destructive habits which will undermine their success. Bad habits catch up with successful people all the time—just look at a newspaper for proof. But the virtues save you from ruinous self-destructive habits.

IV. You are more important than your work

Skills, success and fulfillment are some of the virtues' rewards. Use them regularly and you also gain:

- **The Ripple Effect.** You don't work alone. You have clients, co-workers, customers and an organization that you are part of. Using the virtues helps you act at work in a different way, a better way. This has a positive effect on where you work and who you work with.

- **Clarity.** When you use the virtues, you see clients, coworkers, your circumstances, etc. as they are, not as you wish them to be. Wishful thinking or hiding from bad news ruins careers and organizations.

- **Integrity.** It is highly prized. Leaders look for workers with it, and the virtues give it to you. They give you a clear, consistent code of conduct that you follow at all times. That is integrity.

- **Competitive advantage.** The virtues enhance your talents and abilities, the way getting an advanced degree does. You are sharper, more valuable. You and your organization have gained an edge over the competition.

There is a final reason to use the virtues at work. This is more important than the skills and meaning that the virtues provide, or the other advantages that they bring to you and your organization. It is simply that you are more important than your work. Who you are as a person shapes the kind of life you have, your relationships, your happiness, etc. You spend a lot of time at work, and when you use the virtues at work you are using that time to become a better person. And that is true success and meaning in life.

V. The virtues: What you need to know

Now that you know the benefits of using the virtues at work, why would you hesitate? It's easy to start using them. But you need a little more information first. This section tells you how to use each virtue, what it can do for you, what skills it can give you, and how to know when it has become a habit.

Before you begin, a reminder. The seven virtues are:

1. Compassion
2. Justice
3. Prudence
4. Courage
5. Self-control
6. Humility
7. Hope

Compassion: The most important virtue

Compassion helps you focus on other people. That is why it is important. Success comes from meeting the needs of others and building relationships with them. Compassion helps you do that.

Some people reject the idea of compassion at work. They behave as if ruthlessness, selfishness and grabbing all they can—all opposed to compassion—bring success. Instead, they are weakening the relationships that can produce long-term success. They'll learn when they see the success compassion brings you.

Compassion gives you two skills important to success, relationship building and being proactive. Good relationships are the foundation of success, and they depend on seeing and meeting the other person's needs, which compassion helps you do. And compassion makes you proactive. It gets you to look for ways to help others. This mindset prepares you to act when you see an opportunity, which is an important part of success at work. And compassion makes work meaningful: in order to meet the needs of others, you must put them ahead of yourself. Shifting your focus from yourself to others gives any act—including work—meaning.

There are four Essentials about compassion that you need to know to use it at work:

1. A working definition

Compassion is acting to relieve the needs of others. But your decision to help others must be governed by your reason, not your emotions. That is crucial. It's what lets you use compassion at work—and reap its benefits—without becoming soft.

2. How to use compassion

To use compassion, when you see a need ask yourself two questions: "Can I help?" and "Should I help?" The second question gets your reason to weigh helping against all your responsibilities.

3. The impact it will have at work

Your organization and colleagues benefit also when you use compassion because it helps you:

- Build a work environment that gets results
- Uncover unexpected opportunities
- Take action rather than wait or feel helpless
- Balance competing interests

4. What happens if you don't use compassion

Every virtue protects you from specific self-destructive habits that are easy to slip into. Compassion prevents you from becoming:

- Self-centered—Focused only on yourself. The self-centered are cold, impersonal, uninterested in others and content to leave others' needs unmet.
- Irresponsible—You leave your responsibilities unfulfilled. Your willingness to help others causes you to neglect your duties. You fail those that depend on you.

Finally, how do you know when compassion is becoming a habit? When you frequently:

- Help others when asked, even if it isn't convenient or you don't like them

- Help others without being asked
- Decline to help, even if you can, if helping conflicts with your other obligations
- Take others' needs and circumstances into consideration. For example, you do things yourself when others are busy rather than add to their load.
- Do what you can for people, knowing that trying something is better than doing nothing.
- Make a point of treating others well, remembering that everyone wants to be treated with dignity and respect

Compassion is not religious business, it is human business.
The Dalai Lama

Justice: Everyone sees it

Being just is a quick way to be seen as virtuous. It is noticeable, because every interaction you have with people is either just or unjust. Justice is objective, unlike other virtues, so people know if you are just. And justice is admired and respected, so a little effort on justice pays big dividends.

Justice can bring success because it sharpens your ability to analyze. Using justice gives you skills that help you see through complexity; you are able to find the information you need and ignore distractions. You also learn to apply a framework to that information, so you can use it effectively. Crisp, relevant analysis is the result. And justice also gets you to focus on others and what they deserve; focusing on others adds meaning to your work.

There are four Essentials about justice that you need to know to use it at work:

1. A working definition

Justice is simply giving everyone their due, what they deserve. That's all. Justice won't ask you to give someone more than what they are due. If you give someone more than what they deserve, it might be compassion, but it is not justice. Note--the virtue of justice is not always the same as legal justice. Nor is it always giving everyone an equal amount. These don't necessarily give people what they deserve.

2. How to use it

In any interaction with others, ask yourself, "Is everybody getting what they deserve?" If justice is being done the answer is yes. This simple question focuses you on the key issue. It also fights the rationalizations that can be used to get more than your fair share.

3. The impact it will have at work

Your organization and colleagues benefit also when you use justice because it helps you:

- Build a reputation as someone to work with
- Create loyal, effective teams
- See markets that are dismissed by others
- Develop strong, deep relationships

4. What happens if you don't use justice

Every virtue protects you from specific self-destructive habits that are easy to slip into. Justice stops you from:

- Not giving people what they are due—You shortchange others. You get a short term benefit because you acted in an unethical, unfair or dishonest way. But it will cost you the respect and loyalty of your coworkers. Or worse.
- Giving people more than what they are due— You shortchange yourself and don't get what you deserve. Resentment, anger or a reputation as a pushover can develop.

Finally, how do you know when justice is becoming a habit? When you frequently:

- Notice when others aren't being given enough
- Give everyone what they deserve, even if you want more
- Don't ask people to take less than they are entitled to, even if you would benefit
- Don't let others take from you more than what they deserve, even if they insist

- Don't let feelings determine how much everyone should get
- Don't play favorites

Justice is truth in action.

Benjamin Disraeli

Prudence: The smart virtue

Prudence is the smart virtue. That is, it makes you look smart. It helps you examine your options, pick the best one and figure out how to get it done. Good results come when you are known for doing smart things.

Prudence can bring you success because it helps you make better decisions. It does so by giving you the skills of good judgment and decisiveness. Good judgment comes from using your reason properly and decisiveness from exercising your will. Prudence adds meaning to your work because, as you will see in its definition, it requires you to work for something other than yourself.

There are four Essentials about prudence that you need to know to use it at work:

1. A working definition

Prudence is using your reason to pick the best way to reach a worthy goal. "The best way" is the one that gets you to your worthy goal—or close to it—while keeping potential problems to a minimum. And a "worthy goal" is one that is outside of yourself—a cause, a person, an ideal, etc. It is not self-centered.

2. How to use it

When you are prudent you use three steps to make a decision: you gather information, analyze it—keeping your worthy goal in mind— and decide. Prudence can't guarantee that your decision will work, but it leads you to the best decision under the circumstances.

3. The impact it will have at work

Your organization and colleagues benefit also when you use prudence because it helps you:

- Know when to take action
- Know when to not act and be patient
- Determine when your strategy isn't working and you must adjust it
- Figure out how to make the best of a crisis

4. What happens if you don't use prudence

Every virtue protects you from specific self-destructive habits that are easy to slip into. Prudence prevents you from becoming:

- Foolhardy—Making decisions without thinking them through
- Indecisive—Not making decisions. Maybe because you are over-analyzing, fearful or easily swayed.

Finally, how do you know when prudence is becoming a habit? When you frequently:

- Don't change your mind after making a decision, unless there is new, relevant information
- Tend to get advice before making a decision
- Make an effort to think matters through
- Decide in a reasonable amount of time, before it is too late
- Keep your goals in mind when making a decision
- Don't always follow your first impulse
- Don't get swayed by the latest or most emotionally appealing argument

Chance fights ever on the side of the prudent.
Euripides

Courage: Universally admired

Courage and the courageous are celebrated everywhere. All cultures admire them and the strength and dignity that courage produces. Only some jobs demand physical courage, but all work requires moral courage, a willingness to take a stand in the face of opposition. Admiration and respect will be yours when you demonstrate moral courage.

Courage can help you succeed because it gives you two vital skills: the ability to take risks and perseverance. There is no success without taking some risk. Courage enables you to take that necessary chance and win rewards.
Perseverance helps you carry on when others become afraid. As they quit, you forge ahead. Courage adds meaning to your work too. Those who are afraid focus largely on themselves and what they have to lose. Using courage properly changes your focus from yourself to people and causes outside of yourself, opening you to more fulfillment at work.

There are four Essentials about courage that you need to know to use it at work:

1. A working definition

Courage is taking a risk to do the right thing. Something you value is at stake, and courage uses your reason and will to control your fear so you can take a chance and act. You control fear, it doesn't control you. "The right thing" is what prudence and justice tell you to do.

2. How to use it

If you are reluctant to do the right thing when faced with a situation that involves risk, ask yourself, "Is my hesitation driven by reason or emotion, particularly fear?" If the answer is emotion, do it anyway. That may mean taking action, or it may mean not acting but enduring. But it always means not settling— doing something safe instead of what is right.

3. The impact it will have at work

Your organization and colleagues benefit also when you use courage because it helps you:

- Make a tough decision
- Endure when circumstances are going against you
- Say what needs to be said
- Act when the stakes are high

4. What happens if you don't use courage
Every virtue protects you from specific self-destructive habits that are easy to slip into. Courage keeps you from:

- Cowardice—Knowing what the right thing to do is, but failing to do it. You allow fear to win.
- Recklessness—Not pausing to determine what the right thing to do is or the risks involved; impulses and emotions drive you.

Finally, how do you know when courage is becoming a habit? When you frequently:

- Can identify the right thing to do
- Don't talk yourself out of doing the right thing
- Don't settle or split the difference, unless another virtue signals that you should
- Think of the consequences of acting, and act when you should

- Do what you said you would do, even when it gets hard
- Listen to others, but disregard their advice if it isn't the right thing to do.

Common experience shows how much rarer is moral courage than physical bravery.

Clarence Darrow

Self-control: Build on what you have

Self-control is a crucial element in a successful, fulfilled career. Peter Drucker—the legendary management consultant—came to believe that learning to manage yourself was more important than learning to manage other people. You use self-control already: You don't work only when you feel like it, and you don't ignore assignments you don't like. It may not feel like it, but you are already using this powerful virtue. Build on what you have and reap its rewards.

Self-control can lead to success because it makes you a better worker. It gives you the skills of focus—an ability to hone in on what needs to be done—and discipline—the skill to stay on task. Distraction and procrastination aren't problems for you. Your efficiency and diligence will be rewarded. And using self-control makes it easier to add meaning to your work because it keeps you focused on a person or cause outside of yourself.

There are four Essentials about self-control that you need to know to use it at work:

1. A working definition

Self-control is using your reason and will to moderate your emotions and desires. Emotions are important—your instinct and spirit are partly emotions—but they need to be used properly. Self-control doesn't stifle your emotions. But it doesn't let them control you either.

2. How to use it

Get your reason involved. When your feelings are telling you what to do at work—when they are in charge—pause and give your reason a chance to weigh in. Ask yourself, "Would doing this be smart?" Your reason will guide you.

3. The impact it will have at work

Your organization and colleagues benefit also when you use self-control because it helps you:

- Do what you don't want to do
- Overcome bad habits
- Control your impulses
- Resist pressure

4. What happens if you don't use self-control

Every virtue protects you from specific self-destructive habits that are easy to slip into. Self-control prevents you from becoming:

- Impulsive—What you do depends on what you feel like doing; you are fickle and quit easily.
- Cold and intolerant—You dismiss emotion and human factors entirely. You are overly rational and repressed; unsympathetic.

Finally, how do you know when self-control is becoming a habit? When you frequently:

- Set a plan and stick to it
- Don't let temper, greed, frustration or boredom determine what you do
- Rein yourself in sometimes
- Consider your feelings and the feelings of others, but as only one factor that goes into a decision
- Take a quick pause and think before you react, especially if you are excited, mad or anxious
- Get things done on time

Self-discipline enables you to think first and act afterward.
Napoleon Hill

Humility: See what's really going on

Great things flow from humility. Jim Collins in his best-selling management book *Good to Great*, shows that humility is necessary for exceptional success. With humility you are open to others and their ideas. You can add their strengths to yours and then work really gets better.

Humility leads to success because it makes you more productive. It gives you the skills of delegating and motivating others. When humble, you delegate because you see the strengths of others; you give them tasks that will get the job done and compensate for your weaknesses. You can motivate others because you realize that you need them to overcome your weaknesses. This makes them feel valued and essential, and they are motivated to work hard for you. Humility adds meaning to work because when you are humble you know that you can't succeed by yourself, that you are part of a team. Because you are on a team, your efforts help yourself and your coworkers. Knowing your work helps others brings fulfillment.

There are four Essentials about humility that you need to know to use it at work:

1. A working definition

Humility is knowing and accepting the truth about yourself, your situation and others. It focuses you on reality, what we want to see and what we don't. The humble don't have to put themselves down, as some people think; self-criticism beyond the truth isn't humility, it's stupid.

2. How to use humility

To find the truth about yourself, others and your situation, examine everything from the point of view of an objective observer. This removes your ego and your interests from undue consideration. State both sides of the case and ask yourself, "Which would an objective observer say is true?"

3. The impact it will have at work

Your organization and colleagues benefit also when you use humility because it helps you:

- Profit from the talents of others
- Face up to and tackle problems
- Live up to your responsibilities
- Keep events and yourself in perspective

4. What happens if you don't use humility

Every virtue protects you from specific self-destructive habits that are easy to slip into. Humility keeps you from:

- False pride—You think too highly of yourself and not highly enough of others. This can cause you to criticize others heavily and try to control them.
- Obsequiousness—You deny your talents. You overestimate the abilities of others and defer to them too often. You also stop trying and fail to tap your potential.

Finally, how do you know when humility is becoming a habit? When you frequently:

- Admit that others are better than you at certain things
- Turn to others for help
- Carry out responsibilities that you don't like

- Know that other people and their commitments are just as important as you and your commitments, and you act accordingly
- Recognize that you have talents and abilities that are valuable and you must use them
- Don't blindly accept the ideas or will of others
- Don't spend time wishing circumstances were different; you have a job to do and you do it.
- Don't try to impose your will on every situation
- Admit mistakes

Humility leads to strength and not to weakness.
John J. McCloy

Hope: The fun virtue

Hope is a fun virtue. It makes you sunny and positive. It plays a key role in success because hope tends to be self-fulfilling. Some people don't think that there is a place for hope at work; they believe that hope is soft and just daydreams. Incorrect. They are letting a powerful tool go unused. Take advantage of their mistake.

Hope helps you succeed because the skills it can give—taking the initiative and inspiring others—can make you a more effective leader. Hope drives you to take the initiative; it compels you to strive for your goals. And hope inspires others. They are drawn to the positive attitude and confidence that hope gives you; they see a winner and want to work for you. And hope adds meaning to your work since it helps you envision the good your work can do for others. This spurs you to work for something outside of yourself.

There are four Essentials about hope that you need to know to use it at work:

1. A working definition

Hope is the desire for something good and the expectation of attaining it. But true hope has two traits that prevent it from being soft, wishful thinking. True hope is based on reality—you really can attain the good. And true hope inspires action—you are motivated to go and get that good.

2. How to use hope

You are using hope when you can answer "yes" to three questions when facing a problem or situation: "Do I expect a good outcome?" "Is that realistic?" "Does that expectation get me to act?"

3. The impact it will have at work

Your organization and colleagues benefit also when you use hope because it helps you:

- Delegate effectively
- React strongly to a crisis
- Act when facing an overwhelming problem
- Distinguish between real opportunities and wishful thinking's dead-ends.

4. What happens if you don't use hope

Every virtue protects you from specific self-destructive habits that are easy to slip into. Hope stops you from sliding towards:

- Despair—A conviction that no good outcome is possible. Despair makes you passive, negative and listless.
- Presumption—The certainty that a good outcome is inevitable. You are so sure that you don't try to bring it about. You give control to others, becoming a spectator.

Finally, how do you know when hope is becoming a habit? When you frequently:

- Know that good things can happen, but not by themselves; you do what you can to bring them about.
- Remember that "if you think you can and if think you can't, you are right," and that truth influences how you act
- Look at the world as it is, not as you wish it to be, and then determine what to do
- Don't look for reasons why something won't work, but look for solutions to potential problems

- Think of the positive result of your work and that gives you energy to continue
- Spend more time thinking about the benefits of your work than about the effort you are making

Hope is passion for what is possible.
                              Soren Kierkegaard

VI. How to make the virtues habits

You are on the verge of making work better. You now understand the virtues more completely, and you know the benefits that can come from using them at work: Success; Skills; Fulfillment; Integrity; Competitive Advantage. The final thing you need to know is how to implement the virtues, how to make them habits.

Implementation comes through four, quick steps: Commit, Plan, Do and Review.

1. Commit

Commitment is the key to any accomplishment. When you are committed you are willing to put in the effort that produces results. How do you know that you are committed? You are committed when you give up something now to get something else later. The virtues ask you to give up today's weaknesses and drift toward self-destructive habits so that you will have more skills, success and fulfillment.

Here are two easy steps that can strengthen your commitment:

- Write down why you want to use the virtues. What will they do for you? List all the concrete benefits.
- Think about what will happen to you if you don't use the virtues. Which self-destructive habits will you slide into? Cowardice? Irresponsibility? Is that what you want?

2. Plan

Now that you are committed to using the virtues, make a plan. Plans turn your intention into reality. Plan out how you will use the virtues today. Make your plan something you can do; any intentional use of the virtues helps form your new habit, no matter how small. You don't have to plan anything dramatic.

Here are two easy steps to strengthen your plan:

- Every day pick one virtue to use and plan out how, when, where and under what circumstances you will use it. The more specific the plan, the more likely you are to have success.

- Prepare. Review the four Essentials for your virtue; this will help you see the opportunities to use the virtue hidden in every day events. Especially keep the working definition in mind so you remember what the virtue does.

3. Do

You can't make a virtue a habit, no matter how much preparation you have done, until you Do it, start using it. When you use it, the virtue starts to muscle aside your old habits. To help Do your virtue, establish a deadline by which you will have used your virtue today.

Here are two easy steps that can get you to Do the virtue by your deadline:

- Keep the virtue in the front of your mind. If you are thinking about it, you will see opportunities and you are more likely to Do it. Put up notes, talk about the virtue, look for examples, anything to keep it in mind.
- Be open. Chances to use your virtue that you hadn't planned will appear. When something unexpected arises or you are asked for a favor, that may be an opportunity to Do your virtue.

4. Review

The last step is easy but crucial. Review your progress making a virtue a habit. The Review makes you better at the virtues because you learn which virtues are hard for you, why, and how to make them easier. And the Review keeps you accountable for using the virtues.

Just take a minute or two every day to ask yourself: Did I do the virtue I was planning to do? Yes or no? If no, why not, and what can I do to make sure I do it next time? If yes, was it easier or harder than I expected? Why? And did I see an opportunity to use another virtue? Did I take it? If no, why not?

Here are two easy steps to help you Review:

- Review at the same time every day, for example on your way home from work. Consistency will make it a habit.
- If the Review shows that you did your virtue, reward yourself. It doesn't have to be big, but something pleasant to celebrate a job well done and to keep you enthusiastic.

These four steps—Commit, Plan, Do and Review—are time efficient and yield results. Adopting the virtues will be easier than you think. They are interconnected and reinforce each other; progress using one virtue makes it easier to use the others. And, like using a muscle, the more often you use your reason and will and the more often you make others your focus, the easier it becomes. And the faster work gets better.

VII. Final thoughts

The virtues have improved lives for centuries. People have used them to transform themselves into role models and to make their dreams reality. The virtues are powerful. You can reap tremendous rewards by applying them to your work.

And the virtues don't stop producing good results when you leave work. They affect all aspects of your life. The virtues can strengthen your relationships and make you admired, respected, sought out and successful, inside and outside of work.

Fully implemented, the virtues will give greater meaning to your work. You will have reasons to work that are important and motivate you, like the story of Jimmy Dunne after 9/11. And you can have more success, more recognition of your hard work. People will come to see all that you have to offer. Your ambitions can be realized. As you Thrive 9-to-5, your time at work will be better and your dreams about work can become reality.

Appendix

Which virtue to work on?

Which virtue to work on?

The virtues hold great rewards—more success, more fulfillment from work, integrity, competitive advantages, etc. How do you decide which virtue to develop now?

Read the statements on the following pages. Which describe your actions most accurately? Which identify the way you behave most often? Track your reactions. Note which statements describe you "Frequently," "Sometimes" or "Never." The statements describe actions most of us do occasionally, but you are trying to find those that describe your habits. So pay attention to the statements that resonate with you, those that describe what you do or think or say often.

Review the results. The virtue you should work on, and the self-destructive habits that you are in danger of falling into, will be clear.

Finally, if you find it difficult to decide, just pick one—we can all use the virtues more often.

If many of these sound like you...

1. "Hey, we all have problems; they have to solve theirs."

2. "What can I do? I'm busy."

3. "What they want is a mystery to me."

4. "I am all about making my numbers. People are a cost to be managed."

5. "I am not sure how to help, so I'll wait before I do anything."

6. "I don't care about their issue; I need them to do this for me."

7. "I only get involved when a big problem comes along."

8. "I'll help them now and try to do my work later."

9. "I don't mind finishing it for them again."

10. "I shouldn't do this for you, but one last time."

...then you may need to work on **Compassion**.

If many of these sound like you...

1. "I have favorites, and I try to help them out. I'll give them a little extra or make work easy for them."

2. "I push to get all that I feel that I should have, even if others don't think it's fair."

3. "I make exceptions for myself."

4. "They never understand my situation, so sometimes I cut corners or stretch the truth to get what I want."

5. "I go with my instinct when there is a dispute; I don't have the time to get both sides of the story."

6. "I give people extra because it seems like a nice thing to do."

7. "I make do with less when others insist they should get more."

8. "I always give people what they want—maybe that is why they call me nice."

9. "I don't really make an effort to see things from the others' point of view."

...then you may need to work on **Justice**.

If many of these sound like you...

1. "I focus on issues in isolation. I don't keep my goals in mind when making a decision."

2. "I often do what the last person I spoke to urged me to do."

3. "I frequently put off making decisions because I would like even more information."

4. "I do things that don't seem so smart later on."

5. "I second guess myself all the time."

6. "I make up my own mind; I don't seek much advice."

7. "I pride myself on making quick decisions, following my instincts."

8. "I am all about action, deliberating is a waste of time."

9. "Once I make up my mind, I never change it."

...then you may need to work on **Prudence**.

If many of these sound like you...

1. "Even if I have an idea or something to add I rarely speak up and hardly ever volunteer."

2. "I avoid confrontations or doing something that I know someone won't like."

3. "I tell people what they want to hear."

4. "I would rather split the difference than push for what I think."

5. "If I get push-back or it gets hard to keep going, I'll usually change my mind or agree to stop."

6. "I am action-oriented. I tend to dive right in and not think about consequences."

7. "I go for it. Opportunity doesn't knock twice, and due diligence only tells me what I already know."

8. "I'm risk averse; I back away from doing things that I probably should do because of what will happen if they go wrong."

...then you may need to work on **Courage**.

If many of these sound like you…

1. "I put off doing things that I don't want to do."

2. "I shouldn't but maybe this once it will be alright."

3. "I usually do what I feel like doing."

4. "I get distracted and procrastinate, but doesn't everybody?"

5. "I know I shouldn't be like that, but, hey, that's the way I am."

6. "There often comes a time when I say, "Good enough," and throw in the towel."

7. "I think it is healthier to get mad rather than hold it in."

8. "I don't let people make excuses if they come up short."

9. "I am bottom line and numbers-oriented; I don't go in for coddling people."

10. "I don't suffer fools easily, and I let them know what I think."

…then you may need to work on **Self-control**.

If many of these sound like you…

1. "I am the most talented member of the team, again."

2. "I am constantly correcting others' errors."

3. "If you want something done right you have to do it yourself."

4. "Listening to others is a waste of time; I hardly ever learn anything."

5. "I should be in charge; I know what's going on."

6. "I shouldn't be doing this, it's beneath me."

7. "I don't speak up so others won't see how little I know."

8. "I'll just go along with the others; I'm sure they know better."

9. "I don't like what I have been asked to do, so I'll find a way out of it."

10. "I never apologize."

…then you may need to work on **Humility**.

If many of these sound like you...

1. "I'm on another project that I know won't work out."

2. "When I think of that project or task all the energy drains out of me."

3. "I would like to make that happen, but it seems like a big effort."

4. "If I don't think something will work, I don't pull my weight. Why bother? I have other things to do."

5. "I prefer to look on the bright side, even if it's not very realistic."

6. "Things worked out only because we got lucky."

7. "Things are going well; I don't see any reason to change them."

8. "It will be fine; it always works out in the end."

9. "Any minute now everything will get better, I feel it."

...then you may need to work on **Hope**.

Last question

Do I have a behavior that others object to, but that I explain away, or make excuses for, or make an exception in my case? What virtue would change that behavior?

When you have chosen a virtue to work on and you want the rewards that come from using it at work, read about that virtue's Essentials in Section V "The virtues: What you need to know," and then read Section VI "How to make virtues habits." The four steps outlined in that section— Commit, Plan, Do, Review—will make the virtue you selected a habit, one of your strengths and something to be proud of.

About the Author

Alexander Cummings is a former marketing consultant. He advised some of the world's best known corporations on branding, naming and marketing communications. In addition, Alexander has served as a consultant to non-profit organizations, strengthening their management and marketing. He received his MBA from Yale University and his undergraduate degree from Vanderbilt University.

www.ingramcontent.com/pod-product-compliance
Lightning Source LLC
Chambersburg PA
CBHW071626170526
45166CB00003B/1213